Pebble® Plus

Nocturnal Animals

Bats

by J. Angelique Johnson

Consulting Editor: Gail Saunders-Smith, PhD

Consultant: Tanya Dewey, PhD
University of Michigan Museum of Zoology

CAPSTONE PRESS
a capstone imprint

Pebble Plus is published by Capstone Press,
1710 Roe Crest Drive, North Mankato, Minnesota 56003.
www.capstonepub.com

Books published by Capstone Press are manufactured with paper
containing at least 10 percent post-consumer waste.

Library of Congress Cataloging-in-Publication Data
Johnson, J. Angelique.
  Bats / by J. Angelique Johnson.
      p. cm. — (Pebble plus. Nocturnal animals)
  Includes bibliographical references and index.
  Summary: "Simple text and full-color photos explain the habitat, life cycle, range, and behavior of bats"—Provided by
publisher.
  ISBN 978-1-4296-5286-5 (library binding)
  ISBN 978-1-4296-6190-4 (paperback)
  1. Bats—Juvenile literature. I. Title.
QL737.C5J546 2011
599.4—dc22   2010028682

Editorial Credits
Katy Kudela, editor; Ashlee Suker, designer; Marcie Spence, media researcher; Laura Manthe, production specialist

Photo Credits
Ardea: Nicholas Birks, cover (bat), Steve Downer, 9, Yves Bilat, 5, 13; Minden Pictures: Kim Taylor/NPL, 15,
Modoki Masuda/Nature Production, 17, Takashi Uzu/Nature Production, 11; Nature Picture Library: Kim Taylor, 19;
Shutterstock: Eduard Kyslynskyy, 21, Hugh Lansdown, 1, Rafael Pacheco, cover (moon); Visuals Unlimited: Thomas
Marent, 7

Note to Parents and Teachers

The Nocturnal Animals series supports national science standards related to life science.
This book describes and illustrates bats. The images support early readers in understanding
the text. The repetition of words and phrases helps early readers learn new words. This book
also introduces early readers to subject-specific vocabulary words, which are defined in the
Glossary section. Early readers may need assistance to read some words and to use the Table of
Contents, Glossary, Read More, Internet Sites, and Index sections of the book.

Printed in the United States of America in North Mankato, Minnesota.
112012   007013R

Table of Contents

Night Flight

Bats swoop in the dark sky.

Their wings quietly flap.

These nocturnal animals

take flight while many

flying predators sleep.

Over 900 kinds of bats live around the world. Some form colonies. Others live alone. Bats roost in caves, trees, and other sheltered places.

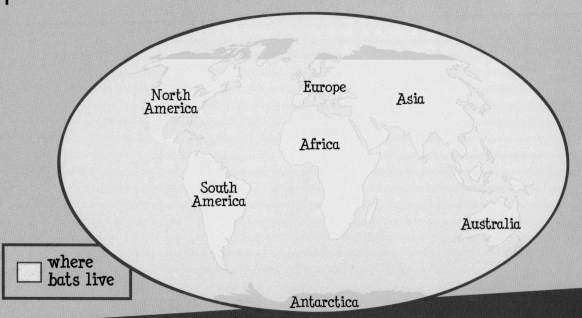

North America

Europe

Asia

Africa

South America

Australia

Antarctica

where bats live

Up Close!

Bats can be many sizes.

Some bats weigh up to

3 pounds (1.4 kilograms).

The Kitti's hog-nosed bat is

as small as a bumblebee.

Kitti's
hog-nosed pup

Bats are furry mammals.

Most bats are brown or black.

Some are red, white, or yellow.

Bats often blend in with shadows

and their surroundings.

Finding Food

To find food in the dark, most bats make high-pitched sounds. These sounds bounce off objects and return as echoes. This process is echolocation.

Bats come out at night to hunt.

Most catch flying insects.

Others nibble on nectar or fruit.

Some bats even catch frogs,

fish, and mice.

Growing Up

Most female bats give birth
while hanging upside down.
They catch their pups
in their folded wings.

Females usually have

one pup at a time.

Mothers nurse their pups

for two to six months.

Pups then learn to fly and hunt.

Staying Safe

To stay safe, bats roost

in hard-to-reach places.

They watch for owls

and other predators.

Some bats live up to 40 years.

Glossary

colony—a large group of animals that live together

echo—the sound that returns after a traveling sound hits an object

echolocation—the process of using sounds and echoes to locate objects

mammal—a warm-blooded animal with a backbone

nectar—a sweet liquid found in many flowers

nocturnal—happening at night; a nocturnal animal is active at night

nurse—to feed a young animal milk from its mother

predator—an animal that hunts other animals for food

pup—a young bat

roost—to settle in a group to rest

Read More

Bekkering, Annalise. *Bats*. Backyard Animals. New York: Weigl Publishers, 2010.

Mattern, Joanne. *The Pebble First Guide to Nocturnal Animals*. Pebble First Guides. Mankato, Minn.: Capstone Press, 2009.

Internet Sites

FactHound offers a safe, fun way to find Internet sites related to this book. All of the sites on FactHound have been researched by our staff.

Here's all you do:

Visit *www.facthound.com*

Type in this code: 9781429652865

 **Super-cool stuff!** Check out projects, games and lots more at **www.capstonekids.com**

Index

Word Count: 205

Grade: 1

Early-Intervention Level: 18